The Unveiling

The Unveiling

Camille A. Frazer

Published in association with CreateSpace.

ISBN: 9780999523001
ISBN: 0999523007

For my mother, Janette,
for her love and sacrifice

Contents

Purpose

Time 1

Dreams buried with the passing of time,
Spent on folly than industry,
Abilities unindulged and unexplored,
Undiscovered.

Hours drifting unawares,
Slowly fading without a care.
Misunderstanding—the disservice to self and community.

Problems waiting to be solved
By abilities still unresolved.
Asleep to the knowledge of our purpose,
Hopefully revived before the final curtain.

Time II

Time, present but silent,
Sweetly, slowly lingering,
Meandering through the day,
Wistful and wandering,
Casual and carefree,
Blissfully passing,
Destination unset.

Time, quick and alert,
Steadily dashing along,
Swifter than the count.
Uncooperative and unyielding,
Unforgiving in its passage,
Fulfilling its purpose.

Time, adds or subtracts,
Wisely forgives and relents.
Teacher to the ready,
Revealer of mysteries woven through the strands
Seemingly waits, hand reaching back,
Forgiving to the one willing to learn.

Time, elusive and insufficient.
Fading to places unknown,
Puttering out the drops of its essence.
Lingering, though not long—
Metered, measured, and exact.
Time, lost.

Self-Life

Here I am, only me.
I have reached the height of my revelry.
Why, isn't this grand!
I have done what I said.
The view is magnificent.
There is nothing to dread.

What say you down there?
I cannot hear;
The wind is rather brisk up here.

This is rather lovely.
But I cannot deny
It's getting quite lonely
With no one nearby.

Perhaps I was too hasty in my ascent.
I forgot to be inclusive—now I lament,
For I have no one to share, no one to cry,
No one to cling to, no one to reply.

Now I must do what I failed before.
I hope they will be forgiving of this old boor.

Tenacity

Tenacity is as tenacity does.
Vital to determine what one will become.

Passion

Excitement hard to contain,
Filled with intensity
Of one's love for his craft—
Unseemly work.

Akin to productive play,
A challenge to improve ideas of yesterday.

Light passes into dark.
Ignorant of time transcending,
Focused on the task at hand.
Desire, burning and unbending.

Guardian's Creed

"I will not be deterred,"
Goes the Guardian's cry.
I have taken up a mantle,
One worthy and dignified.

I will not be silenced
Like the children under my watch.
Too long they suffered.
My mission will not be latched.

I will investigate.
I will uncover.
I will recommend.
I will endeavor
To ensure it's safe for them to return—
Or to find a new home altogether.
To find the strength within themselves.
To return, never.

Opportunity

Opportunity knocks once, per chance twice.
It is for us to recognize
The signs as they come in.
Be aware, dialed in.
Be ready when they arise so
That our dreams can be realized.

Opportunity knocks;
Open up, and let it in.
And so, begin.

Grit

The list was long—
So much to do.
Procure, lift, move.

A packed schedule seemingly difficult to complete,
But for uncommon will
And help from the Father,
Who, like no other,
Opened a window to fulfill.

Discipline

What bother it is to fix the mind,
To do and follow through, despite protest.
'Tis the way to overcome,
Push through to become
The one I long to be—
A better me.

Ying and Yang

Opposites,
Yet one mission:
Improve the human condition.
Restore sight to eyes years dimmed
From cataracts that reduced their living.

One quiet, with measured, precise steps,
Spurred by young loss ne'er will forget.
Left his humble life for Indian shores
To return with skills so his kin will suffer no more.

The other, energy bursting in leaps and bounds,
Conquering hills and foreign mounds.
Inspired by the work of the quiet one,
Escaped the bustling city for quiet lands.

Doctors performing their rounds
On villagers from faraway towns,
Who walked for miles with family,
Those same, long unseen.

A small slit,
The cloud removed.
Lens inserted,
Sight improved.

Such little cost
For so priceless a gem.
They ensure sight is restored again.

What a scene to behold—
The faces when they see,
The surgeons with hearts of gold,
And the smiles of their families.

Titan

A giant among men,
Clearing paths and blazing trails.
Going against the odds,
Daring to be denied.

Uncommon in approach,
Striking out on lonely roads.
Uncertain of that which lies ahead
Except certainty.

Present

Here I am, in this moment.
Just as I am, me.
Attuned to my thoughts and being,
My shortcomings and feelings.

It won't help one bit.
An escape to forget
My challenges and complexities
They are, but part of me.

I will do the work in this little room.
Focus on the good in me that others see.
Be kind and forgiving, present and healing
And take the time to just be.

Fracture

Misguided

I live in wealth.
My friend, you live in poverty,
Devoid of love and empathy,
Disconnected from your purpose to yourself and fellow man.
To live in service and improve while you can,
Your kin, earth, and sea,
To lay aside all propensity,
To gain at costly expense
And provide no recompense
For harsh words and selfish gain,
Until little remains
To the injured one who but can say,
"So it is for those who have lost their way."

Sabotage

I care not for my fellow man,
So I advance my own interest.
Why should I be mindful of anyone else?
Be at their behest?

I want what I want.
Why should I consider you?
The fault is your own
That you didn't better choose.

My destiny is my own.
I chart my own course.
Such foolish talk; no man stands alone.

What is it I have done?
'Tis not what I yearned.

Yes, see you harmed yourself.
I pray you now learn
To sometimes forego self-interest
And stand with your fellow man
That no man stands alone,
That no man is an island.

Lost

To lose one's soul for but small gains
Is insignificant to the one disconnected from God.

Who fails to see his brother,
Only his wants
And marches to the beat of that drum,
Drowning out the noise of the oppressed.

Never a thought of the consequence to others,
Interested only in achieving personal gain.
Lost to good vibrations,
Audience of one.

Forest for the Trees

When will we see the forest, not just the trees?
Will it be when Mother Earth brings us to our knees?
I do so doubt, as we oft repeat
The same atrocities our fathers committed centuries ago,
Which our children will also know.

But for the members who rise above
In charity and brotherly love,
We would go down in history
As another generation who missed the forest for the trees.

Bittersweet

Indulge in me get your fill
Of the layers of my milky sweetness.
Let me erase your hard day, sadness, and worry.
Savor the complexities of my flavor,
Blissfully unaware of the labor of:

Children lured and kidnapped like slaves of old
By countrymen plied by riches untold,
Who through ignorance or greed
Barter the future sent on ships on wheels.

Unripened dreams snatched up and snuffed out,
Replaced by machetes
For chopping ripe fruit with succulent centers.
Parched later like their pickers,
Unable to escape the deep forest,
Earning nothing except their keep.

Fearful and powerless,
With no ability to communicate the horror, except
The drop from their brow,
The stain of their eyes,
The blood from their hands,
The emptiness of their hearts
In bittersweet chocolate.

Atrocity

'Tis no living for the faint of heart
Nor the stout either.
Picking cotton, cutting sugar
Till fingers be blistered.

They say I am black and can bear it.
But oh, how the sun does tear at high noon.
No less strenuous when it goes down.
Though it don't lash me so,
And I but bear a bit once more.

Education

Education
Essential, but perhaps not the kind daily administered.
Rote repetitions,
Rehearsed for tests,
Hardly of value
To pass life's test.

Teach of honesty,
Teach of drive,
Teach of the urgency of time.

Teach of character,
Teach of respect,
Teach how to decide to lessen regret.

Teach of integrity,
Teach of heart,
Teach of situations never to depart.

Teach of enterprise,
Teach of tact,
Teach of traits not found in rote books.

Social Irresponsibility

Ne'er a thought of the consequences of the defeat within.
Not a result of untried error
But a launch of known sin.

Lies that cover
Unbecoming endeavors.
Greed to line pockets by flawed designs
That sharply kill,
Slowly poison
And separate families from one another.

Will you ever care?
Will you ever learn?
Or are you too distracted by the wealth generated from a lack of
social concern?

Death of Common Sense

Bins overflowing with food within
Discarded
Otherwise edible.
Death of common sense.

While hunger abounds onshore and off,
Longing for relief
From food lying wasted in bins.
Death of common sense.

Deforestation

For the felling of its trees, the forest groans.
Memories uprooted.
Cleared for palm oil and soy beans,
Lucrative industries.

Less clean air with each one down.
Plenty of carbon monoxide to go around
To stifle vulnerable tribes and communities
And kill local commodities.

Fruitless effort planting trees
To replace those of centuries
Of rooted networks that keep the soil
From tumbling down the hillside.

Too late for the lives lost
To brown mud and competing costs.
Voices silenced as they cascade down
Like trees, once renowned.

Shackled Life

Number 8243,
That's how they refer to me.
Shouted, marked off,
Nothing but a number, another loss.

Bars clanked
Trays slammed,
Minds thought empty, but full.

Memories too painful to remember
Pushed back by the hardness within.
Shackled by time and circumstances
Sometimes too hard to overcome.
But still, we press up and press on,
Hopeful of a change, redemption, and acceptance.

Stocks and Trades

Gather near to hear
Of the old, once again new—
A story so outrageous
It hardly rings as true.

Of men filled with natural pride,
Caught and stripped thereof,
Chained and bound,
Caged and placed in stocks.

Carried to northern shores.
Bartered, traded, and shamed.
Worked and whipped all day through.
Injustice compounded and renewed.

To a time of disguised reprieve—
Free to do as you please
Till the crows, unsatisfied,
Change the law to soothe their pride.

So kings of men
Return again
To modern cages,
Placed in stocks and traded.

Vexation

Oh, what vexation fills my soul
To see the injustice meted out.
Chained, impaled, raped, and whipped
For sport.

What right think you to possess
To so address?
A people regal and free,
To now display on trees!

Think on what it says of you.
The truth, not some justification imagined and rehearsed,
Repeated across generations as a memory verse.

Think on what it does to your soul,
Betwixt one and thirty-nine.
I imagine there be an ounce of guilt,
Though not enough to relieve my kind.

Hidden History

Stories rich
Still yet uncovered,
Distinct from the running narrative.
Lives of wondrous accomplishments
Hidden.

Until we write our own stories
That tell of remarkable glories.
Contributions too numerous to count
To lift our heads and come about.

'Tis the lesson to take away.
He who tells the story rules the day,
So tell your stories, my people, well,
And you shan't be hidden again.

Health Scare

Scared to die,
Scared to live,
While men legislate on Capitol Hill.
Scared to die, as there is no money to pay
Embalmers and workers to dig your grave.
Scared to live a life of meager means
Of lack, of no redeem.

Tales of visits with little wait
In respectable facilities of goodly state.
Affordable remedies that stand to cure
Ailment, maladies, and sick woes.

All at universal expense,
Where in earthly life there may be no recompense,
Save for contribution to the health and well-being of your fellow
man.
Herein lies honorable health care I can understand.

Shell Game 1

How shall we do this so they don't see?
The real meaning of our intentions
How do we deceive?

Have you seen the trick of sleight hands?
Move the ball around with dizzying speed.
Cover here, shift there.
That's how our plans will be achieved.

That is just what we will do.
Create friction and spread it thick.
Divert their attention,
While we burn tradition to the wick.

They'll never know our plans
Until it's too late.
And they can't do anything about it
Despite how grave.

Shift

Stand still and hear the change.
The wind blows a different way.
The warm sun has dimmed.
Winter is here.

It comes slowly,
Gathering the elements of its nature,
Testing the remnants of the warmth.

Then it strikes with a blistering force
While attempting to soften the blow
With whispers of necessity,
As everyone ought to know.

It cuts and slashes,
Blisters and rehashes, oiled skins
Slathered in self-interest.

But the sun will not stand the cold.
It marches through the sky,
Pushing back the dreadful clouds
Threatening to bring complete awry.

In time, it warms the hearts of cold men,
Now that they can see again
And understand how wrong they had been
To have let the cold in.

Faith

The Moon

Bright shines the light upon the crater below.
Alone, wondering, what became of the magnificence of man, hon-
orable once before,
Now distracted by the darkness,
Hopeful of their return to the glow.

Rebirth

The falling away of self brings forth life.
The fruit will not awaken and bear until the tree is culled.
Each pruning ushers new growth.
Self is revitalized when it is pruned of dead matter.
It is a necessary evolution of the soul.

Shell Game II

See how they move at dizzying speed?
Creating distractions, covering their sleeves?

Something is afoot
Though not clear.
Be on the lookout.
Things are not as they appear.

They think themselves clever,
Fumble, then pardon.
Be not deceived.
They seek to test the water.

I see the vibration!
The ripples are clear.
They thought themselves too clever.
I see it all, very clear.

Lionhearted

Who knows the heart of a champion?
Stout against seemingly insurmountable odds
Unwilling to be counted out,
Determined.

The race seems long.
Time is no friend.
The champion fights on
Undeterred.

Clear head,
Fixed eyes,
Steady hands,
Victory!

Fray

Frayed at the seams
Unraveling with each added pressure.
Ill equipped to handle the demands,
Shackled by knowledge unknown for generations.

On whom to depend?
What to do?
Why does this happen?
When will it end?
Where can I learn that which I need?
Who will help?
In me, will anyone believe?

Plagued by the questions anew,
Still uncertain what to do.
Can't digest all I am told.
Hard to unlearn habits of old.

But must do what I can.
New eyes look to me each day
For food, shelter, a new way.
So I do the steps to keep it together.
Recite new lessons until I remember.
Which keep the seams from unraveling further,
Frayed, but knitted forever.

A Warrior's Heart

I will not break.
I will not bend.
I will be fierce to the end.

I will not be silenced though you try.
Others will take up the mantle
You seek to deny.

I will be tireless
Though sometimes weary.
To quit would be contrary.

Eyes of steel
Set fixed on the prize.
Mind determined
That justice must rise.

Faith

Lord, You said You would make it great,
So why do I hesitate, to believe unquestionably in Your promise?
Keep me strong in my belief,
And increase my faith as I wait.

Assurance

My dear child, why do you grieve?
In Me firmly believe.
I will deliver you from your trouble in due time.
Don't worry your head, nor bother your heart.
I have not forgotten you are mine.

Hueman

How different you look.
How small your eye.
How strange your nose came the reply.
Your hair so curled, while mine straight.
Here are differences one can't negate.

Yet we know:
Laughter we know.
Pain we know.
Love contains the same.
We know sadness.
We know grief.
We know time brings relief.

Herein similarities lie
That hue cannot deny.
We are one if we will see
One humanity.

Humanity

I am you, I am me.
I am he, I am she.
I am they, I am us.
We are one, thus.

Hope

Refugee

Tempest and trials in my homeland,
Home despite destitution and strife.
Clinging to hope of change
Until hope buckles under reality.

Mind and heart
Determined to overcome the journey ahead.
Passage negotiated,
Separated from family unable to survive.

Braving cold, heat, land, water.
Heart numb, but steeled.
Feet blistered, but determined.
Terrain hard, but welcomed.
Sea perilous, but with possibility.

A new shore
Brimming with hope of a new life.
Helpers and workers,
Welcoming or not,
Checked in and placed
In crammed homes, jungles, and hotels.

Final destination or stopover,
That hopefully delivers on the dream,
Though nostalgia visits hometowns and cherished memories.
Perhaps one day to be better relived.

Free!

Basking in the morning sun
In a grove by the avenue,
Rays of glory drying the dew
Of the mist.

Head raised over the cluster,
Watching cars go by
Green, red, blue,
Admiring my golden radiance.

Suddenly, stirs then panic
In the brotherhood.
Ladders mounted,
Hands grappling,
One, two, three we go,
Tossed in a truck below
Bound for steam city.

What to do, but despair.
Gloomily gaze on life passing by.
Until a screech and a jerk,
A tumble and fall,
And off I go rolling down the avenue far below
To a spot in the field,
Watching greens, reds, and blues
And feeling free.

Fields of Dreams

Bend, toil, twist, turn.
Touch, inspect, accept, deny.
Pull, pluck, cut, snap,
Place, package all that.

Break, stand for a few.
View the rows left to do.
Wipe the beads.
Pull the hat.
Straighten the gloves for a spat.

Then:
Lift, walk, carry, release,
Until the vines are appeased.

'Tis the life for now
One of generations of old,
But new ones matriculate
Into new fields of dreams to behold.

Perseverance

Who knew what I would become
When I was but a wee lad,
Skipping stones and telling jokes,
Dreaming of far-off lands?

They hardly knew that beneath the mask
Stood a boy with a vision,
Motivated by legends on high
To halls of but a few.

Not perfect, but improving,
Not yet successful, but undeterred,
Sometimes doubtful, but persistent,
Keeping the dream alive.

Until the gift is perfected.
The artist catapulted
To far-off lands afore imagined.
A dream more realized than contemplated.

Hotel Clerk

What do you do while patrons sleep?
Do you study, wander, or pray keep
Watch over your charges with monitors on high?
Or read of worlds far away thus far denied?

Savored Sacrifice

Who would have known, looking at us in grand chairs,
That once we labored in fields and groves?

Immigrants from lands afar
Forced to flee with no more than family.
Lives abandoned,
Hurts pushed aside.
Thoughts of failure never to abide.

Dreams built with steadfast hands,
Mindful ever of the prize.

Now,
As we look on our legacy
Children grown and accomplished,
We look on with content
Of lives well spent
Creating another dimension,
Times over to be mentioned.

Manna

Sacks of food descend from the sky
To waiting mouths below.
Barely enough to meet the need,
Meager to satisfy the grumbling foe.

Hearts destitute, ravaged by war,
Fight against a travesty on par.
Orphans devoid of kin stay near to swift feet,
Bare bones against slight skin
About to fill out on milk meat.

A fight not just by fleeing men
But caring hearts willing to lend a hand
Across borders and aisles
That send rescue planes in the skies
To drop sacks of food to waiting mouths
Until no longer necessary or the next war comes about.

Return to Sender

It is fascinating to know not to whom you go
Or the relief you bring to a grateful being.
You are released, and your path is charted to where it must end.
The extent of your gift surpasses where it began.

Regal

Think of the former days
When the world wondered at the eloquence and intelligence of an
unlikely son,
One who won warm hearts with the possible dream of "yes, we
can"
And restored admiration around the world for a country that wel-
comed its members with a beacon.
Camelot evident once more.

Battled and undermined,
Challenged with contempt,
Obstructed and belittled,
Pursuant to plan.

Still, unswervingly dignified,
Rising high against the tide.
Proud and accomplished,
Elegance personified.

Regal II

Hard metal beneath soft veneer,
Stands a maiden
Fit for the task, ready.

Regal beauty poised beyond measure,
Wisdom and intelligence suitable for the endeavor,
Daughter, mother, wife, First Lady.

Love

What Is Love?

Is it the excitement that builds with your smile?
Is it your breath on my skin that makes me go wild?
Is it the touch of your hand while laced through mine?
Or the warmth in your eyes that burns with desire?

Surely, it's the grasp of your hand around my waist,
The caress of your fingers on my face,
Your sensual kiss as we hold embrace
By the clear blue sea.

Perhaps, it's your grace forgiving an err,
Your quietness amid the stir,
The understanding you share
Or assurance in times of despair.

Yes, it's your presence ever near,
Your laugh that fills the air,
A heart forever true.
My love, you.

Courtship

Where did you go?
Days of making acquaintances and house calls
With permission from parents before long walks.

Of letters filled with poetry and prose,
With scents of perfume,
Or the gift of a rose.

A time of measured words
If one's heart was unsure,
Careful not to give the wrong impression
Of a pairing you will forego.

Of stout hearts and soft eyes
Of sweetly held hands and finally the prize,
Of a companion to have and to hold,
This was courtship of old.

Perspective

"Thank you for calling."
What did she mean?
Dismissive, uninterested, am I of no redeem?
What was I thinking?
She's out of my league!
How I even got her number
I scarce believe.

Back to my place
The one I belong.
Best stay there now.
Can't go wrong.

She's calling again
For reasons unknown.
Dare I hope?

"Hello, sorry about earlier. I didn't know what to say.
I was nervous and panicked and in such disarray.
Here's what I really want to convey."

Shock, disbelief.
Could this be true?
Funny how my thoughts went far afield of what she knew.

Love Letters

Bated breath awaits
The ring of the postman
Riding down the avenue
Toward my door.

Will this be the day he stops and alights,
Delivering you to me once more?

Alas, the familiar script
Ever so faithful,
Pressed to my bosom,
Cherished.

"I love you more than my letter before.
I miss our walk by the stream.
I can't wait to see you, my dear,
Until then I dream."

The words will sustain until we unite.
I read them once more with delight.
Pen to paper I take to send
By way of the postman when he comes again.

Love Me

Love me fierce.
Love me calm.
Love me tender.
Love me warm.
Challenge,
Acquiesce,
Bring out my very best.

Love me long.
Love me deep.
Love me hard.
Love me meek.
Be my lover.
Be my friend.
Love me to the very end.

Devotion

My love for you will never fade.
From you I will never depart.
I will love you with a fearless love,
One that requires my whole heart.

You are my entire being.
I think of ways to please you more.
I gaze upon you unknown
From the place at your side.

I will love you through the hard times.
When we don't know what to say,
I will sit with you in silence
Until we find our way.

I will walk this life with you.
I will hold you in my hand.
Reminisce of a time before
Of the place my love began.

Commitment

I am pleased to meet you, the love of my life,
My eternal partner, my soon-to-be wife.
I have loved you for so long,
Even before we met.
Give yourself to me, and you will never regret,
The life we will share together,
The memories of our start.
Give your heart to me, as from you I will never depart.

The Old House

Packed in boxes ready to ship
Are memories of your old bones
Creased with lines of laughter
And times of less mirth.

You came to me small and unassuming,
Quietly standing atop the street
Shaded by a majestic oak,
Hiding your treasure within.

An area for a garden
To beautify and attract
The wonders of nature
Flittering by.

Your rooms though small
Are peaceful within
And tell no tale
Of times before.

They lead to an outdoor wonder,
Screened from the creek on high,
Land eager to yield pleasures galore.

Oh, I will miss this old house,
Per chance time will allow me to enjoy once more.

Slumber

Get ye sleep into the abyss.
At least for a session more
That I may rest in the deep.
And my dreams be in keep of the gentle Master.

Watchful over His charge,
Peaceful and unalarmed,
Quiet to the world without
And time bustling about
Until the touch
Of the Master's hand
Awakens and enlivens
The senses to life.

Earnest

On a quiet street
In a quiet land,
A man walks the way
With generosity flowing from his hands.

He picks litter from the shallow creek to keep it clean,
Rolls garbage bins from curbs to yards before owners stir,
While softly whistling
So they are undisturbed.

Such charity and love for his fellow man
That he looks among discards to send to foreign lands.
They say one man's trash is another man's treasure.
The fullness of this heart is beyond measure.

For the Love of the Game

Balls spinning back and forth
In the deuce and ad courts.
Serves at dizzying speeds
The most amazing volleys ever seen.

Herein lie the joys of tennis
From the lawn of Wimbledon to the clay of Paris.
Champions of yesteryear mentoring younger talents,
Champions in their own right,
Williams, Federer, Bryan, twice.

A singles sport saves the chance.
You are matched with a partner well versed in the doubles dance.

Event Planner

Drapes cascading from the ceiling to the floor,
The work of the busy matron to and fro from her station.

Peppermint balls affixed all around hand-frosted snow globes.
Memories arranged with precise skill
To be played to delighted thrill.

Days of work tapering down.
Another successful event for a talent renowned.

Boss Lady

Busy as a bee, she goes bustling about
Organizing, putting fires out.
Attention to detail she gives everything.
To avoid subsequent misgiving.

Always a step ahead,
Above the curve.
One wonders if we truly deserve
The wealth of ethic and expertise,
Of which we are so well pleased.

Princess

Curls tightly spun descend in sun-kissed spiral hues,
Springing with step as if on cue.
A cover for a head intelligent and wise.
Soft as the heart, in everyone's eyes a prize.
A little girl no more, a young lady now.
On her way to the wonderful woman she will become.

Peeny-Wallie

Light then dark goes the night,
Proving such delight
To the lad keen with interest
In capturing one of nature's best.

He walks with his jar to and fro
Unsure of where the firefly will next go.
His aunt says, "It's getting late."
Leaving without his prize, he cannot contemplate.

He walks crestfallen to the house,
Jar empty, face to the floor.
How can one deny this quest?
Back out for a spill.
Who knows, maybe he will.
Capture a light fleeting and free
And fill the face once more with glee.

It seems doubtful, but wait,
The lid opens and mitigates the disappointment thus far.
A light briefly emitting inside the jar.

Mother and Daughter

Who is this child I see?
A tad different from the one who grew inside me,
Who came out and clung to my breast,
Who now longs to leave my nest.

So different from the toddler with tight curls,
Who hung on my feet and pulled my skirt.
The one who bravely let go the first day of school,
Unlike her mother, subject to ridicule.

Is this child in front of me who banged on keys in elementary?
Then played beautifully at recitals
To cries of encore.

Yes, 'tis the child matured to a young lady.
No longer at my feet
No longer a baby.
Intrigued more by makeup and friends' advice,
Doubtful her mother's is good, having lived no life.

If only she knew what I do so well,
One day she will likely possess the very traits she hopes never to
experience again.

The Lord

A day to reflect on the sacrifice of the King,
A Man like no other.
Who left paradise for earth below
And paid a price, the value we may never know.
He lives today, restful till when
It's time for His return again.

Beauty

Hibernation

Deep in burrowed brown
Sleeps a bulb hibernating in winter.
Covers pulled,
Free from clips and cuts, pulls and dust,
Until the time it lifts its head to spring's welcome.

Spring

Your day is set,
And it's good to see
The burst of seeds out in revelry.
And such a welcome surprise
By an earlier greet,
When frost gives way
To clogged feet that hoe, spade, lift, and hike
Throughout the season to bring delight
To home and onlookers alike
Of the splendor of spring so keen to excite.

Awakening

Safe and sound,
Secure within,
Still dark in the cocoon of my skin.

Leaves rolled away, as if on cue,
To usher my arrival after the morning dew.

Sun on my dress,
Welcoming wonder.
Softened by trees, gazing yonder.

Time now, I can no longer delay.
I open with splendor to greet the day.

Ole Man Winter

On second thought, I think I will stay,
Howl a bit more; make you rue the day.
You said I lingered past my prime,
That it was Groundhog Day and it was full time.
I gave way to awakening bulbs in the Sunshine state.
Too bad, ole Phil saw his shadow, and dear lady spring will have
to wait.

Garden Goddess

She stands in the yard
Hands akimbo,
Spade jotting out, rich with dirt.

She digs to give the fruits of her labor,
Sucklings from the island
Scarce to find.

Memories galore
Of times before
Of moments beneath trees
For shade while basking on golden glories.

It is a joy to give from her nursery
Plants from back home,
Through which moments can be lived once more.

Authentic

There is no question of who you are.
Your essence shines clearly through.
The air is light when you are around.
Your nature rings true.

There is no pretense.
In your presence
No fear of ill ease,
As you are at peace
With your very being.

Beautiful Isle

A land ideal,
A beautiful isle
Descending into criminality,
Being ruined of its pride.

It wasn't an overnight descent.
Nay, a slow erosion,
Departure from tradition
To the ways of the Romans.

Families fractured,
Mannerisms undone,
Children unattended.
What will they become?

Will the land lose its luster?
Or will the people muster
The strength to push against the tide
Of that which seeks to override?

Morning

The sea kisses the shoreline
Softly in the morning,
Greeting the grainy sand
Along the beach.

The banter of the early breaks
Comforts the waking hearts
Stubborn to rise
For want of slumber.

The ocean meets but more,
Raising its tempo along the shore
Joined by the strides of the committed,
Disturbing the meeting of old friends.

The River

To the river we go,
To wash and to play.
Ne'er mind it's far away.
Passing the time skipping and singing,
Trying not to fall behind those on a chore.

Finally, the sound of gushing water,
A peep of wet stone on the bank,
Then full view of the majestic dam.

Wash, lather,
Pitter, patter,
Rinse, dry,
Swim, dive.

A bit of work,
A bit of fun,
Mission accomplished
For everyone.

Nature's Call

Softly rising in the early afternoon
Comes the call of the sparrow,
Singing sweetly of the passing clouds
That had covered its joy.

Flittering from tree to tree,
It swells with abandoned glee,
Telling tales of the glorious sun
And of the day won.

The Wind

The wind moves between the trees,
Unseen but evident by their sway to and fro.
The rustle heightens to a crescendo
Spurred by tempestuous blows.

Errand

The trail leads down a winding path,
Loose stones scattered along the way.
In the distance, the call of a pup unattended.
The sound lingers,
Faint now against chores.

Young daises caught in the wind
Sway their heads to and fro.
Carefree and cheerful, content nowhere to go.

Finally, the clearing straight and solemn,
Fixed stones of cobble
Echoing the clatter of industry,
Distinct from the village.

Grazing

Grazing on the brown
As the rain pours down,
The cattle eat their full,
Oblivious to the shower.

The young calves romp around,
Trotting between the elders,
Ignoring their charge,
Hooves splattered with dirt.

Room with a View

A window to the world outside
Thinly veiled from within.
Playful birds flitter by,
Perching on places unseen,
From where they sing and squeal.

One stops at the window below,
As if it knows
The mistress watches from the screen.
She pulls the curtain ever so slight.
But, alas, too much for the keen bird who takes flight.

Vinyl

The crackle of your sound
Brings memories of old
Like wood in a fire.

The smoothness of your vinyl
Round and dark
Eliciting songs of enjoyment.

What temper you bring
To a hurried world beat
As you slowly wobble and spin.

Bird on a Wire

A bird on a wire sings a song
Of glee and joy as pedestrians pass along.
Perched on a wire so slight,
It raises its tune in sheer delight,
At the breeze cool this early morn
And the glory of its sojourn.

The Magic of Music

Music soothes the soul.
Takes hold of, makes you sway.
It ministers and enlivens
Captures, enraptures.

It stirs old memories,
Spurs revelries.
From the start of the rhythm to the end of the riff,
It wraps us in its magical gift.

Sunday

The hum of the mower cuts into the solitude of the morning,
Disturbing turning heads on lush beds and slow saunters
Partaking in light reads and joyful kneads for secondary pleasure.

Even birds usually alight
Have taken a slow start from the night.
Still resting in warm nests and hollowed trees,
Ignoring the intrusion of the one with perspiring beads.

Splendor

What content it is to lie
Upon your lush evergreen.
And gaze upon the sky above
On this clear day.

What more could one contend to partake but this?
A day by the river,
Silent on the bank.

Is there more to be satisfied?
I would be mystified
That there be more than this.

Showers

What welcome sound you bring,
Streams of rain cascading down the roof,
Soothing the hearts within.

There be no better thing to hear
Than the cadence above as we draw near
Windowsills and pillow tops,
As we listen to your comforting drops.

Songbird

Tweet, tweet, tweet.
It goes with each beat,
In sync with the flap of its wing,
As it flies merrily to the next spot from which to sing.

Mimosa Piduca

No one's here.
Ah, such relief.
I dread it so, people touching my leaves.

I think it gives them joy.
To me, it's a terror.
My nature, you see, is oh so tender.

I am shy and sensitive.
Stare never.
I rather me you not remember.

Here comes one
What a big fellow!
Hand outstretched, how it bellows.

He shakes so hard,
I doubt I will recover.
I close up shop, until perhaps tomorrow.

Afternoon Song

Two birds on distant trees
Engaged in sustained chitter speech.
One tells of cool breeze and light air,
The other agrees in sweet melody, "Same here."

Their voices atop solo chirps and caws
With reports of playful children and mirthful paws,
Of the magnificent this afternoon seen
In the park by the stream.

Venus

I got you now!
You will never recover.
From my grasp, you will soon discover.
The chamber you thought sweet and rosy in color
Is a trap under cover.

I saw you alight,
And I prepared,
In case you touched my hair unaware.
You did not once, but twice,
So now you are my prey.
In twenty seconds, you shall be lunch today.

I wish I could grant you a reprieve.
But 'tis my nature you see.
Forgive my manners as I tighten while you move.
Try as you might, your fate can't be improved.
I am sorry this news is hard to bear.
But you had your chance before touching that second hair.

Escape

I see you watching as I move about your rosy chamber.
Without a shadow of doubt,
You will not catch me today I do pledge,
I am stealth and slim and move aware within.

Oh, I caught a hair.
I best be clever
And not touch another as I would leave here never.

I saunter about feasting on your few.
Mindful of what you are preparing to do.
Your leaves once relaxed now perk with attention.
No sense in prolonging this contention.
I bid you adieu. I will not be lunch today.
Forgive my manners and my uneventful stay.

Meaning

Charity

How beautiful a purpose,
How remarkable a feat
To give of oneself
To help fulfill a dream.

Life is more than possessions.
There is such meaning
In sharing with others
And showing there's still much to believe in.

Charity begins at home.
It springs from the heart.
It touches the giver and the receiver.
A good virtue to impart.

Mindfulness

Be still in the moment.
Observe its lingering visit,
Certain of its nature,
Quiet and unobtrusive.

Be present in the moment.
Aware and enlightened,
Detached from misconceptions
Of the simplicity of mindfulness.

Still

Be quiet, my soul,
Amid the swirling questions,
The unknown abyss.

Recall times past,
Similar challenges faced.
Know you will find your way.

Back to your center, your peace, your place.
Awaken, my soul,
Settled, reassured.

Stand

Consider your feet and where they go.
Look before you leap, as advised of old.
Follow not men who entice,
With stories of fortune from "innocent" vice.

Be keen to the still small voice,
Beneath the bellow of alluring choices,
   ·   That counsels to not haste,
Forsake a path that ends in sordid fate.

Consider your feet and where they go.
Better to stand where certain than go.

Soul Searching

Oh, soul, where art thou?
Thou no longer cling within me.
You are far away; I feel you not.
You were strong in tranquility when I knew the essence of my
being.
Time spent in charity,
Enjoying the beauty of this creation.

You slipped away unnoticed
When I looked without.
I search for you now in the places you were with me last.
Searching, hoping, finding.

Be Revived

Darkness all around.
Seek the light.
Unburden yourself from the foreign.
You were not made for this.

What does it profit to struggle all alone in the density of the dark,
dank smog?
Be revived to your inheritance.
Be lifted from the fog.
Enter into the clear
Where you rightfully belong.

Reason, Season, Lifetime

You entered unassumingly
And fit neatly in a space as if always there.
You offered laughter and friendship.
For a challenge, advice you shared.
In retrospect, that was the reason you appeared.

You lingered long,
According to your time,
Through hills and valleys,
Faithful by my side,
Until the years waned, and before I knew,
Your season passed too.

You are here with me today.
Through it all, you remained.
Whether near or far away, you have stayed.
To help with a reason,
In and out of seasons,
Forever—for a lifetime.

Change

Things seldom remain,
Whether good or bad.
Life ebbs and flows like waves rolling in and out.
So too life's subjects are at times tossed about.

The answer lies in the response.
Fight or flight, stay or go—
It may be more apt, rather,
To go with the flow.

Transition

In your last moment, you will know how you should have lived.
It will be clear that life is best lived in love, kindness, and sharing
that which you can give.

That friendships should be nurtured and not abused.
That people are not objects to be used.
That moments with family are to be considered time well spent.
That there is an art to communicating that minimizes confusion
of what is meant.
That there is equal import of hard work and enterprise,
To rest and gaiety to avoid a soul's demise.

That the world is larger and is to be explored.
That it will reveal things in your proximity unknown.
That love pure in form has no formidable rival to overcome its
persistence unbridled.
That the glories of the world once held dear
Mean nothing at the end unless they were shared.

About the Author

Camille A. Frazer has been staunchly defending the rights of children since 2005. She was born in Jamaica and currently lives in Florida, where she works as an attorney specializing in child welfare.

www.ingramcontent.com/pod-product-compliance
Lightning Source LLC
LaVergne TN
LVHW041225080426
835508LV00011B/1085